Through Sickness and In Health
– *How to Survive Your Spouse's Mental Illness*

By: Tami Dickerson
Edited by: Timothy Kline

TABLE OF CONTENTS

The information in this book is not intended to substitute for professional psychiatric care. Please be sure to seek a board- certified psychiatrist if you believe your spouse is suffering from psychiatric issues.

A Word From the Author

Before anything else I want to make a confession: Although I am a health care worker, and I often times work with patients who have psychiatric issues, I do not work specifically in the psychiatric field. That being said, how can you know that I know what I'm talking about in this book? Because this book is specifically written to help people who are married to psychiatric patients, and I am one who is married to a psychiatric patient.

I have been through the horror of realizing that my own husband had developed mental illness. I've been through the frustration of my own ignorance, wasting time trying to find help in all the wrong places. When I finally stumbled onto the right path I learned the process of finding the best treatment to fit my husband's needs. And all along the way I learned the requirements, the treatment options, and the bumps in the road to beware of as we worked to restore my husband's mental health.

I know this journey well – and it was made more difficult by the sheer fact that I didn't know where to start or how to get there. I wrote this book as a guide in hopes of sparing you those same, frustrating, difficulties.

Chapter 1
Overview of Mental Illness

I presume you are reading this book because you have realized – or are suspicious that – your mate is suffering from some form of mental illness (a.k.a. psychiatric illness) Perhaps you married your spouse without realizing that he or she is suffering from some form of psychiatric problem (it can happen). Or perhaps you already knew the person has a psychiatric diagnosis but you married anyway because he or she has been successfully stabilized through treatment. Or, as in our case, perhaps you married a person who later developed psychiatric issues long after your wedding day. Perhaps your situation is in a unique category altogether.

Regardless of *how* it happened, it is important to realize that mental illness is as much a physical problem as mental. It is not something that a person can just "snap out of" anymore than a person can "snap out of" cancer, arthritis, or a kidney infection. Many people don't realize that mental illness is actually a physical problem within the brain that causes an affected mental state. What do I mean by this? Let me explain:

The brain's ability to think and reason is completely dependent upon the balance of physical chemical exchanges that are required for normal, functional thinking.[1] If any of these exchanges become chronically disrupted the patient's brain will begin to lose its ability to process thoughts or information correctly, resulting in a case of psychiatric illness. The longer the disruption is allowed to remain the worse the patient becomes because the issue cannot correct itself, just as cancer, arthritis, or a kidney infection cannot correct itself. Just as physical illness requires medication or other treatments in order to restore normal physical health, and psychiatric illness likewise requires medication or other treatments in order to restore mental health. This is why it is imperative that mental health patients receive proper treatment as quickly as possible.

What causes the onset of these chemical disturbances? Sometimes such disturbances run in family genetics. Sometimes it is caused by a severe head injury.[2] Sometimes it can be brought on by alcohol or drug abuse. Other times it can be caused by severe or prolonged emotional trauma[3]. In yet other cases it can be a case of hormonal issues. And in some cases, it can even be caused by certain physical ailments or diseases. Because the reasons are many and varied, the treatment options are likewise many and varied.

---

1   For purposes of simplicity, "chemical exchanges" includes hormones, vitamins, minerals, enzymes, proteins and other compounds needed for normal brain function.

2   A head injury can interfere with the exchange of chemicals, depending upon the severity and location of the injury.

3   Because emotions are based on the physical chemical exchanges, severe or prolonged emotional difficulty can disturb the balance.

Whatever your situation is, this book is written to help support you *and* your marriage as you journey through your spouse's illness together. It may seem like an overwhelming situation in the beginning, but rest assured that there *is* help and treatment for your spouse that can restore him or her to a mentally healthy state.

This book is designed to help you understand the process as well as the resources available to help you and your spouse navigate the road to wellness.

Chapter 2
Seeking Help For Your Spouse

The first thing you need to know is that a proper diagnosis of psychiatric illness requires the expertise of a board-certified psychiatrist, which is *not* the same as a psychologist or a counselor. Many people confuse these professions, so let me define the differences for you:

- **Psychiatrist:** A board-certified psychiatrist is specially trained in the assessment, diagnosis, treatment and prevention of mental illness. It is a medical degree in which the professional must first learn to be a medical doctor before continuing on to specialize in psychiatry. Because they are medical doctors they can prescribe medications.

- **Psychologist:** A psychologist's primary focus is on a patient's thoughts, feelings, and general mental health. They are *NOT* trained to assess, diagnose, treat or prevent mental illness.

- **Counselor:** Counselors and therapists have education similar to a psychologist. Ergo, they do not have a medical degree, nor are they trained to assess, diagnose, or treat mental illness.

Although psychiatrists and psychologists have different scopes of practice they will oftentimes work together in treating a patient. However, in order to get a valid diagnosis you must start with the psychiatrist first. This was something that I only came to realize after wasting a year and a half in approaching our own situation from the wrong direction.

For us, the road towards understanding and addressing my husband's mental illness began when I found myself no longer able to ignore the unpleasant changes in his personality: His sleeping habits were becoming erratic, he began losing interest in some of his favorite past-times, and his usually calm demeanor was becoming more easily agitated. Eventually I made time to privately discuss these things with him and he told me that he was feeling bouts of agitation welling up but he didn't know what to do about them or how to control them. He wasn't becoming violent at this point, but clearly there was something very wrong happening. At this point we'd been married for about thirteen years, so we were well acquainted with one another's habits and idiosyncracies – this was certainly something new developing.

Later, when I was alone with my thoughts, I pondered the possible causes for his developing issues. I found myself remembering a severe car accident we'd been involved in just after our tenth wedding anniversary. Both of our young sons nearly died from their injuries, and my husband had a severe head injury along with other severe injuries. As for me, I was lucky enough to walk away with only three broken ribs. I remembered how my husband was in the hospital, slipping in and out of consciousness for the first 24 hours after the accident. Could the head injury have had a delayed effect? Or maybe he was experiencing Post Traumatic Stress Disorder as an after-effect of the accident? We discussed these possibilities and decided that perhaps seeing a counselor would help him. Since my job at the time offered free counseling through an Employee Assistance Program ("EAP") we started with that and signed up for family counseling.

Our first counseling session with the EAP counselor was also our last: At the end of the session the counselor decided our main problem was that my husband was unemployed at the time and a job would fix most of his problems. My response to the counselor's suggestion was "Seriously? I've been with this man for over a decade and seen him through unemployment periods before. This is *NOT* a simple case of the no-job-blues!" Strike One.

My next move was to look in our local yellow pages for a family counselor. We found one who advertised that she counseled with a Christian perspective. Since we are a Christian family we thought we may have better results with her and so we set up an appointment. We continued to see her for several months. During this time my husband's condition worsened: Not only did his agitation increase but he was also starting to become suspicious and paranoid about others' actions, including the actions of strangers. He was also starting to read things into everything I'd say, no matter how nonsensical it was. Because I didn't realize that a counselor is *not* specially trained to assess or diagnose psychiatric issues I expressed concern to the counselor that maybe my husband had PTSD[4] or some form of depression. In response she asked him three simple questions and then determined that he neither had depression, nor did he have PTSD. Although I'm no professional in mental health it didn't seem like three quick questions should be enough to determine such things. Strike Two.

After two failures with counselors it took me several weeks to muster up the courage to seek another one. However, my husband wasn't getting any better and I was at a loss of what else to do. So, again I went to the phone book and looked through the listings. This time we chose a secular counselor and signed up for family counseling with her; we saw her for six months. She wasn't bad, but it became clear to me over time that my husband's problems weren't a matter of mere counseling. My husband's agitation increased to the point that the tiniest thing would set him off – and we didn't always know what that "thing" would be until it triggered him. He was getting to

---

4   PTSD is **P**ost **T**raumatic **S**tress **D**isorder.

the point that if he saw strangers talking to each other he'd insist they were talking about *him*. He was also developing unreasonable suspicions towards my older son – his stepson. We'd discuss these things with the counselor, and she seemed to listen, but to no avail – she continued to conduct the counseling sessions without any change. My husband's agitation was growing to the point that he began destroying property in our home. His hair-trigger agitation and growing paranoia were beginning to scare me *AND* the kids – and yet the counselor didn't have alternative recommendations or ideas for help? I was seriously contemplating canceling our sessions with her when the final straw happened:

My older son, who was by now fifteen and in that obnoxious stage teens enter during that time in their lives, happened to be on the phone and was trying to peek at a Christmas present my husband bought for me. My husband's reaction was to grab the phone out of my son's hand and smash it to pieces, then tackle him into a card table, which then gashed a hole in the wall. As if that was not enough, my husband brought the ordeal to a finish by pouring a two-liter bottle of soda over my son's head. Although my son was physically unharmed the look on his face bespoke the emotional injury, and I realized that whatever was behind all of this, it was now way out of hand. My husband, in his skewed reasoning, didn't see anything wrong with what he'd done and couldn't understand why I was so upset about it. He felt that he was in the right and didn't understand why we didn't agree.

Since this happened during my son's Christmas vacation from school, and not knowing what else to do, I immediately contacted my son's paternal aunt who lived out of town, and asked if she'd take him until we could get my husband figured out. My son's biological father was deceased and she was the first choice I had. On New Year's Eve my son moved in with his aunt, where he stayed for the next several months. Meanwhile, my younger son (who is fathered by my husband) remained with us. Since my husband's wrath seemed to be targeting my older son I thought it best to get him out of the line of fire while I tried to figure out the next step. Between the lack of results from the sessions with different counselors, and my husband's explosive behaviour, I was at my Strike Three as far as counseling was concerned.

Since none of the counselors mentioned anything about going to a psychiatrist, and I still didn't know that there was a difference between them and psychiatrists, I didn't know what else to do. I was hoping that giving my husband and my son a few months of time apart would help calm things down. In the meantime I began confiding in some of my co-workers at the hospital I worked in. Maybe they'd have some insight or advice I could use, surely I couldn't be the *only* one who's ever gone through this kind of thing.

Most of my co-workers advised me to "kick him to the curb" and "pack his stuff and kick him out". And, I have to admit, I was seriously tempted to do it. I hated the dark, brooding, paranoid stranger he had become – where was the cool guy that I married and lived with for all those years? It became like walking on egg shells around him. *BUT....* I married him "for better or worse" and "in sickness and health". And I just knew the *REAL* husband, the man I married, was in there *somewhere*. I still believed he had either severe depression or PTSD, but after three counselors I felt lost and didn't know what I should do next. But I did know that if I gave up on him now I'd never get him back.

As I aimlessly went day by day feeling lost and helpless, watching the man I married sink deeper into his whatever-it-was, our relationship felt torpedoed. And then the bombshell happened:

It was the "new normal" for a typical day: My older son was still living with his aunt, and our younger son was in school for the day. I was at home with my husband walking on eggshells trying to steer clear of him, and him being the exasperatingly paranoid, dark, brooding stranger. I don't even remember what sparked it now, but he said something that seriously annoyed me and I just blew up at him. I couldn't take it anymore and I screamed at him, and he reacted by knocking several pictures off the wall, shattering glass everywhere. I strongly protested his actions, and he responded by picking up a large shard of glass and forcefully pressing it into his own wrist! I wrestled the glass away from him, cutting myself in the process, and called 911 emergency, telling them my husband was trying to hurt himself. The cops and the ambulance came, and he was taken to an out of town hospital that had a "Behavioral Science" unit. I couldn't go with him because first I had to get our young son from school (he was only nine years old), knowing that if I went with my husband I wouldn't be back in time for our son, and I certainly didn't want him locked out of the house. Because I had only a driver's permit at that time I was dependent on a ride to take us to the hospital. By the time our son and I actually arrived at the hospital (about 90 minutes later), the hospital was ready to release my husband. I realized that my absence hurt the situation: They had only his word to go on; without my input they didn't have any reference point. As a result he was being released.

I spoke to the hospital staff about our situation and that's when they *strongly* recommended that I schedule a psychiatric evaluation for my husband at the county mental health clinic. When I informed them that we'd already been through three different counselors, *that's* when I was finally educated about the differences between psychiatry, psychology and counseling.

If only I had known there was a difference before this, I would have done it long before! I was outraged that the counselors we saw never even *mentioned* the possibility of a psychiatrist or evaluation! I was outraged that the second counselor never admitted that she wasn't trained to assess or diagnose mental issues! Looking back on it, it was obvious that his issues were *far* beyond the scope of what they could help with – and they should have recognized this at some point during our sessions! Seriously, I – a person not educated in mental health issues – recognized something of it; how could *they* have missed it?!

Don't get me wrong, I am not against the idea of counselors and their counseling. They are very valuable professionals who help many people get through their various problems in life. *HOWEVER*, I strongly recommend that if you think your counselor isn't "doing it" for you, that you bring up the topic of psychiatric issues. Any counselor worth your money will *not* be offended and will help you explore the options.

At this point I must state that you should first evaluate the reaction you may receive from your spouse when you bring up the idea of a psychiatric evaluation. Depending upon your spouse's state of mind, he or she may take it well, or may not. Seriously consider how delicate this situation may be because you do not want to alienate your spouse any more than is necessary. Some spouses will be okay with it, but for others it may be wiser to have the counselor broach the topic with your spouse. If your counselor is unwilling to discuss these things in private with you then I recommend contacting a psychiatrist directly and discussing the situation with him or her. You can find listings of psychiatrists in your local phone book, your local mental health clinic, your local hospital (especially if the hospital has a psychiatric unit) or your local psychiatric institution.

When you make your first appointment to see the psychiatrist, he or she will need specific information about your spouse's condition and symptoms. Here are some some of the things the psychiatrist will be needing to know:

- What are the specific changes you have seen in your spouse?
- Is your spouse experiencing severe mood swings?
- Is your spouse experiencing hallucinations? (Hallucinations aren't always visual, they can involve any of the five senses).
- Has your spouse's sleep habits changed? Has his or her sleep become increasingly disturbed?
- Has your spouse's hygiene habits changed?
- Has your spouse's work habits changed?
- Is your spouse becoming increasingly violent or agitated?
- Has he or she become withdrawn and/or moody?
- Is there an increase in paranoia? Does he or she think others are against them?
- Is your spouse becoming increasingly easy to startle?

- Does your spouse have a history of drug or alcohol use?
- Is your spouse becoming delusional?

Of course, there may be more information that the psychiatrist will need, but these will give you an idea of where to start. Be honest with the psychiatrist and don't omit things no matter how embarrassing, weird, or scary they are. The doctor cannot properly help your spouse if he or she doesn't have complete information.

After you've had the preliminary discussion with the psychiatrist you need to schedule a comprehensive psychiatric evaluation, a.k.a. "psych eval" in order to get an accurate diagnosis of your spouse's illness. Such evaluations are very thorough and take more than one session to complete. Although you may be impatient and want to get the ball rolling quickly, it is essential that the evaluation examines every detail, otherwise you may not get a proper diagnosis, resulting in the wrong treatment. Therefore, you may find yourself scheduling two or three days of sessions within a single week in order to finish the evaluation. This is a time when patience is a virtue.

So, of course, the next question is: What happens during the course of a psychiatric evaluation? A comprehensive evaluation can vary from doctor to doctor, but they have similar components (This is just an example, there may be other angles investigated depending upon the individual case) :

- A description of the disruptive behaviors and patterns that the patient displays as well as noted symptoms.
- Effects of the patient's behavior/symptoms in relation to their employment, schooling, relationships, family members and leisure activities.
- The taking of a complete family medical history including physical and mental health issues as well as current medications or treatments – this includes any use of herbal treatments, over the counter remedies, naturopathic remedies, homeopathic treatment, prescribed medications, etc.
- The effects of any recreational use of drugs or heavy drinking.
- A one-on-one interview between the doctor and the patient.
- A roster of various lab tests to determine if there are underlying medical conditions.
- A discussion of any traumatic events that may have been experienced during the patient's lifetime (abuse, trauma, emotional problems, etc.).

After the doctor assesses the results of the psychiatric evaluation it is extremely important that family members and friends be as supportive as possible towards the patient. It has been proven that treatment has a much higher success rate when the patient has a close knit support network with people who know and love them. The doctor will expect this and will make him or herself available for your questions and reassurances throughout the treatment process. Once a diagnosis has been made it is equally important to go along with the treatments prescribed by the doctor. Please note that no two cases are identical, therefore treatment options will vary on a case by case basis. The doctor will also depend on you to let him or her know if you notice any adverse side effects of the treatments, so make sure you are aware of any side effects you should look out for.

And now, for the million dollar question:

What if my sick spouse *refuses* to get a psychiatric evaluation and/or treatment? What do I do *then*?

First, you need to realize that a diagnosis is sometimes more scary for the patient than it is for the healthy spouse. Most people do not want to carry the labels of "mentally ill" or "psychiatric patient." The social stigma associated with these labels can be very distressing to the patient, and thus he or she may try to avoid anything that would stick that label to them. In other cases the patient may truly believe that he or she is mentally healthy and that *you* are the one who is sick. And then there are some who may believe that you are conspiring against him or her with such notions. What do you do with a spouse who refuses help?

Unfortunately there isn't a quick answer to this mainly because each case is different. In some cases you may be able to alleviate your spouse's fears by continually assuring your spouse that you still have respect for him or her, and that you intend to be as supportive as you can. Assure your spouse that his or her diagnosis will not become public knowledge. Some healthy spouses even go so far as to get their own psychiatric evaluation at the same time as the sick spouse as a show of solidarity. Of course, such an approach may not work in some cases – this can be especially true when the sick spouse is experiencing severe symptoms. Then what do you do?

If your sick spouse is a danger to himself or to others you should be able to get your spouse committed to a psychiatric institution regardless of his or her agreement; this is known as involuntary commitment. It may sound mean, but it's not – it's a necessary process in order to help your sick spouse become well. If your spouse is too sick to recognize his or her need for help you will need to step in and provide that help. And yes, it can be a very emotionally trying experience for both you and your spouse, but your spouse will not get well if he or she does not get the necessary treatment.

In order to commit your spouse you must obtain a court order from a judge that commits your spouse to a mental institution. Laws governing involuntary commitment vary between states and across international lines, so I strongly advise you to contact a local psychiatrist or local legal agency in order to learn how to go about this procedure.

When a patient is involuntarily committed they are generally held for a certain period of time – usually 3 to 5 business days – in which they are observed and evaluated by a psychiatrist. The outcome of the observation and evaluation dictates any resulting treatment or release. Therefore, it is extremely important that you give as much input as you reasonably can.[5] If you don't, then the evaluators will have to act on only partial information; and this could be detrimental to your spouse's chances of being mentally restored.

---

5   In other words, don't be a pest. Give as much information that they ask of you, of course – but don't insert yourself unnecessarily into the process. Ensure that they have your contact information in case they need more information from you later.

Chapter 3
Your Relationship With Your Spouse

Confirmation that your spouse is mentally ill can be a devastating event. You will find yourself wrestling with a mixed bag of emotions and uncomfortable thoughts, and this is to be expected. You may feel any combination of sadness, anger, frustration, fear, and embarrassment. You will likely have reservations about maintaining a sexual relationship with your spouse now that you know that he or she is mentally ill. You may even feel overwhelmed to the point that you fantasize about running away. However, if you abandon your spouse or make yourself emotionally distant you will cause your spouse more distress, resulting in his or her condition to worsen. If you don't help your spouse seek treatment, who will? But, how can you be supportive when you're feeling overwhelmed? The fact is, you will not be able to face this mountain alone. This is where a network of family and friends' support is as important for yourself as it is for your spouse.

Unfortunately, some people do not have the luxury of having friends or family as a support network for several reasons. Perhaps the potential supporters are in denial of your spouse's condition, or perhaps you've just moved to a new location and your supporters are now long distance. Perhaps something happened in your life that has estranged you from your family and friends (perhaps even your spouse's past behavior has done this). Take heart, you still do not need to be alone in this situation:

I strongly suggest that you discuss support options with your spouse's psychiatrist. Your spouse's psychiatrist can inform you of local support groups and meetings for family members of mentally ill patients. You may also find online mental health support forums to join. Another option is looking into faith-based support groups in your community – check around with your local houses of worship. You may also opt to find a counselor in your local yellow pages who can help you work through your feelings of distress. Just be aware that it isn't rude to try out more than one counselor; you are seeking a good rapport with a good counselor, and sometimes that takes more than just the first try. Remember, you *must* take care of yourself if you are going to be in a position to help your spouse.

Another point that gets missed is this: It is very likely that your spouse will be equally devastated by an official diagnosis. The spouse may fear that he or she is defective or that you will abandon the marriage. Your spouse may be equally embarrassed by the diagnosis, and may even feel unworthy of your love or validation.

And this is where it gets very delicate for *you*: Your spouse deserves to get treatment and be made well again, and you – as the life partner – will be the main person your spouse will lean on during this emotional period. This is the part where you need to figure out how you can give him or her support without wearing yourself out in the process.

Here is some advice that helped me when I was faced with this issue:

- Everyone's situation is different. You cannot expect a certain result based on someone else's experience.

- Be sure you do not withdraw emotionally from your spouse. Your spouse may feel very sensitive about losing you at this beginning stage, and that's a common and valid fear.

- If you are comfortable with maintaining a sexual relationship with your spouse then by all means do so, it'll help reassure your spouse of your intention to stick around. If, however, you are *not* comfortable with sex at this stage, I strongly suggest speaking to the psychiatrist or a counselor on how to best handle the issue. Realize, though, that this is no excuse for you to start an extramarital affair.

- Continue your daily routine. Part of regaining the health of your spouse means keeping the routines you've had and shared as much as reasonably possible.

- Your spouse may need a lot of reassurance at this time. Be sure to let your spouse know that you are committed to helping him or her regain mental stability. Hold your spouse's hand, give hugs generously, and be sure to listen when he or she wants to share fears and feelings with you.

- Do not be easily discouraged by your spouse's reactions to receiving a diagnosis. Everyone reacts differently, and you cannot expect a "normal" reaction from someone who's thinking ability is impaired.

- Realize that, once treatment starts taking *full* effect, the ultimate responsibility for your spouse's treatment is your spouse. Although you may need to give reminders for appointments or the taking of one's medications, especially in the beginning, you are not your spouse's parent. Once the spouse begins thinking more clearly then the spouse needs to actively participate in his or her own treatment.

The main point is to give your spouse unconditional love as you both climb this mountain together. It will not be easy in the beginning since treatment hasn't yet actually begun. And once treatment begins you cannot expect overnight miracles for two reasons:

1. It can take anywhere from six months to a year to find the correct medication and treatment combination that best suits your spouse's needs.
2. Many psychiatric medications take at least four weeks to reach full effect in a patient.

As I've stated before, when it comes to treatment, patience is a virtue.

It also must be said that, in some cases, the sick spouse's behavior may become so difficult that he or she may need to live outside the home while treatment begins – especially if his or her behavior is affecting your children. This can mean the spouse may live with a supportive friend or relative, or it may mean institutionalizing the spouse. You're right, none of that sounds wonderful, but this isn't about comfort, this is about getting your spouse the help he or she needs while protecting your family from further negative or violent behaviors. This is something that should be discussed with your spouse's psychiatrist, your counselor, or even a trusted congregational leader.

In our own case, after his release from the hospital Behavioral Unit, I was too afraid of my husband's behavior and I had to make the painful decision to order him out of our home. At that time his sister owned a gift shop in another city, and he ended up staying on the couch in the back storage area of the shop. If you find yourself in the awful position of having to live apart from your spouse, assure your spouse that you are *not* giving up on him or her, and that the living arrangement is merely temporary. Reassure your spouse that your goal is to help him or her get well and reunite as a family, and that you'll do whatever it takes to help that happen. Of course, your spouse's reaction will depend on whatever the illness is. If and when this subject is broached, it will help if it's done within a safe and neutral environment so that your sick spouse does not feel "ganged-up on" or "attacked".

If you find yourselves needing to live in separate places ensure that your spouse does not feel abandoned by you. Schedule regular phone calls and/or visits, preferably on a daily basis if at all possible. If it can't be daily, then find some kind of regular schedule that works, *and stick to it*. Use email and texting if you can. If your children are comfortable with it, then be sure to include them in the calls and visits also. Keep the visits for as long or short a time as is comfortable for you and your children, but keep it consistent. Try to get at least an hour in each time, maybe longer, if possible. It is vital that your spouse knows that you aren't giving up – this is a very trying time for your spouse too, don't forget that.

There may be times when a sick spouse may refuse your calls and visits. Do not let that discourage you. It may be that your spouse is feeling like a burden to you and wants to relieve you of the burden. Perhaps your spouse is angry with you because of the situation, especially if he or she still does not recognize the need for treatment. In spite of your spouse's own thoughts and conflicted emotions, keep your call and visit schedule anyway while you wait for treatment to start taking effect. If you are still refused, write positive and encouraging letters to your spouse, and include your kids' artwork or letters as well. Remember, until treatment takes effect your spouse will not be thinking or reasoning clearly, and it is *not* your spouse's fault. Once the treatment begins to work he or she will remember that you still tried and that you didn't give up. That will be priceless in your spouse's mind.

It is also important to remember that your spouse needs to be treated as an *adult* during this time; you are not your spouse's parent so do not treat him or her as if a child. How can you know the fine line between taking care of the spouse and becoming the "parent?"

Taking care of your spouse includes accompanying him or her to appointments, ensuring your spouse has his or her physical needs met, and keeping companionship with the spouse for as much as is reasonable. You are stepping into "parenting" territory though when you start hovering over every little thing he or she is doing, continually nag at your spouse, or try to use negative reinforcement (punishment) to modify your spouse's behavior or activities. Yes, it may be extremely difficult to refrain from falling into the parent-mode, especially when you want to take control of the situation, but realize that falling into it only hinders your spouse's healing process. Right now your spouse needs you to be his or her best friend, not a parent. If you find yourself unsure of whether you are stepping into the parent mode discuss this with your support network, the psychiatrist, your personal counselor, or trusted congregational leader in order to receive guidance on the matter.

Chapter 4
Family Implications

The implications of a psychiatric diagnosis stretch beyond the husband-and-wife relationship: There are also children, extended family, and in-laws. It is almost a given that there will be family members who refuse to accept that one of their own has a psychiatric problem. There may be some who believe your spouse is just "going through a phase" or can just "snap out of it". Some believe that psychiatrists are nothing but quacks.

Realize that denial stems from many things: Fear of family stigma, embarrassment if the condition becomes common knowledge, and the simple act of "wishing it away" are all common reactions. It is very uncomfortable to think that a family member has a psychiatric illness, therefore it is a tough concept for some of them to accept. In some cases, some may even accuse *you*, the healthy spouse, of "making it up" or lying about the matter (this actually happened to me). Sometimes people would rather believe *anything else* instead of accepting that one of their own has a psychiatric diagnosis.

Don't let those nay-sayers derail you or your spouse. It is a proven medical fact that mental illness is caused by an imbalance of the chemical processes in the brain, and only proper treatment can restore that balance. Believe me, your mentally ill spouse is no worse than anyone else with some other heath issue: He or she is no worse than a cancer patient, or a heart patient, or an accident victim. It is neither your fault nor your spouse's fault that he or she is suffering from the condition. If a family member or a close friend is unable to accept the diagnosis, then you need to simply back off and give those ones time to adjust to the idea.

Remember, many of them were probably unaware that your spouse has been experiencing a decline in mental stability. As the healthy spouse, you probably didn't complain or mention the growing problems to other family members for any number of reasons, so the diagnosis may come as a complete surprise to them. In our own case we don't live in the same area that my husband's family lives, and I didn't say much about his mounting issues in the beginning. Therefore, when he began to seriously fall apart it was a complete surprise for them.

It is helpful to remind them that a diagnosis of mental illness is no different than the diagnosis of any other illness. It is not a "death" sentence, nor is it always a permanent condition. It may also help to know that there are many famous people who've successfully managed their mental health issues with proper treatment, people such as:

1. **Buzz Aldrin**, famous astronaut. With proper treatment he was able to manage his severe depression.

2. **Richard Simmons**, famous diet and exercise guru. Successfully managed his ordeal with anorexia and bulimia with treatment.

3. **John Nash**, famous mathematical genius and Nobel Prize winner. Successfully managed his paranoid schizophrenia with treatment.

4. **Brooke Shields**, famous actress. Successfully managed to pull out of her severe post-partum depression with proper treatment.

These are just a few of many. There are numerous people, right now, all over the world who are able to function normally and make valid contributions to society due to treatments which restored their mental health. Mental illness *can* be managed and lives *can* be restored with the proper treatment; don't let anyone convince you of the opposite. If, in spite of your best efforts, certain ones continue to cling to their denials, don't waste your time and energy on proving them wrong. You need to focus on your spouse and your children more than you need to focus on someone's inability to accept a difficult fact.

And now we need to talk about your children: Your children's ages will dictate how much information you share with them about your spouse's condition. Obviously, a very young child will not understand as much as an older child. When very young children see the sick parent acting in strange or scary ways they need a simple explanation: *"Daddy has a sickness that makes it hard for him to think clearly. Mommy found a doctor for him who'll figure out daddy's sickness and give him the treatment he needs to make the sickness go away."* is plenty of explanation for very little ones. Older children can be given more concrete explanations depending on their age and maturity level.

Realize that your children will be anxious about the whole thing; mental illness is not as easy a concept to understand as physical illness is: A child understands a fever, or vomiting, or a stuffy nose. It's harder to understand a sickness that messes with one's thinking and reasoning abilities. A child may fear that he or she may catch the illness from the sick parent – reassure the child that it isn't a germ he or she can catch; instead, it is a matter of a body part (the brain) not functioning correctly, and that a doctor can help make the brain work better. Assure your children that the sickness can be treated, and that the sick parent can get better; it will just take a little time.

During this time your children may have a difficult time knowing how to deal with their own emotions on these matters. Some children may become withdrawn, some may start having trouble in school, and some may start "acting up" at home. Some may develop sleeping or eating issues. Many will display a combination of these negative behaviors. It is extremely important that your child's emotional well-being is addressed, even if these behaviors don't show up immediately. There is no shame in taking your children to see a child psychologist, school psychologist or counselor in order to help them sort through their fears and feelings at this time. I also strongly recommend that you let your children's teachers know what's happening so that they can offer any help or services that may be available in the school or the community as well.

Chapter 5
Variations of Mental Illness

Mental illness comes in a variety of forms. Some of them include (this is not a full listing):

- **Anxiety Disorders:**
    Obsessive Compulsive Disorder
    Disassociative Identity Disorder
    Post Traumatic Stress Disorder
    Generalized Anxiety Disorder
    Social Anxiety
    Phobias
- **Mood Disorders:**
    Post-Partum Depression
    Clinical Depression
    Bi-Polar Disorder
- **Eating Disorders:**
    Anorexia Nervosa
    Bulimia
    Pica
- **Psychotic Disorders:**
    Schizophreniform Disorder
    Schizoaffective Disorder
    Psychotic Depression
    Delusional Disorder
    Schizophrenia

The number of different possibilities is the main reason why a psychiatric evaluation is so thorough and takes so long; the doctor needs to be able to find the correct diagnosis. Each psychiatric disorder manifests itself differently in each patient, so often times it is difficult to pin it down unless you have a thorough evaluation. And sometimes, as in my husband's case, a patient can be suffering from more than one diagnosis at the same time. In fact, my husband seemed to have hit the jackpot: He was diagnosed with *three* – depression, PTSD, and a form of schizophrenia!

Let's discuss the various disorders listed on the preceding page:

ANXIETY DISORDERS:

Obsessive-Compulsive Disorder, also known as OCD, causes a patient to be stuck in an endless, repetitive cycle of thought and behavior. Such patients are hounded by recurring thoughts or fears which make them perform their obsessive rituals in an attempt to make the thoughts or fears go away. This condition can waste many hours of a patient's day as he or she repeats the obsessive behavior throughout the day. For example, a patient may feel the need to avoid stepping on all sidewalk cracks; if he accidentally steps on one, he may feel the irrational need to go back to the start of the sidewalk and begin avoiding all those same cracks all over again. The patient may realize how senseless the compulsion is, but he or she is unable to refrain from doing it anyway.

Disassociative Identity Disorder is sometimes known as "Multiple Personality Disorder". It is thought that this disorder is a coping mechanism originating from trauma caused by abuse endured in childhood – physical, sexual, or emotional abuse. The disorder serves to remove the patient from experiences which are too traumatic for the patient to accept in the conscious mind. The number of "personalities" in a patient varies from case to case and these personalities may not match who the patient is. Each personality has its own unique identity and may vary in gender, age, ethnicity, religion, etc. Each has its own mannerisms, postures and speech patterns. Hypothetically, this means that a straight, Catholic, Latina patient could harbor a personality who is an atheist, white, gay, man. In some cases the various personalities are aware of each other, and in other cases they are not. In many cases it can take years to diagnose because the symptoms may look very much like other psychiatric conditions.

Post-Traumatic Stress Disorder can be triggered when a person experiences an extremely terrifying or traumatic event, such as war, sexual assault, severe accidents, unexpected death or a terrifying disaster. Patients suffering from this disorder tend to have terrifying thoughts or memories associated with the trigger event and usually show a high level of emotional numbness.

Generalized Anxiety Disorder presents as extreme anxiety and worry about everyday events without any obvious reasons for the worry. Such patients always expect disaster and oftentimes will not leave their homes for fear of what might happen "out there." The worry and anxiety becomes so prominent that it interferes with the patient's everyday functioning.

Patients with *Social Anxiety* are afflicted with an overwhelming fear of social situations. They fear being judged by others and fear ridicule. Such people will avoid parties, places of worship, and any place in which people tend to gather, such as a public beach, a park, or a carnival.

Phobias are unreasonable fears of objects, places, or situations. For example, a person may have an extreme fear of water, and thus may not shower, shave, wash clothing or their dishes. Phobias severely restrict a patient's quality of life and well-being.

MOOD DISORDERS:

Post-Partum depression is caused by the sudden upheaval of hormones that occurs immediately after the end of a pregnancy. This can occur after child birth, miscarriage, or elective abortion. It is caused when the pregnancy hormones fail to re-balance after the pregnancy, which directly affects the woman's brain chemical function. Although this doesn't happen to all women, it is not an uncommon affliction. In some extreme cases the post-partum depression becomes so bad that the new mother becomes delusional, resulting in post-partum psychosis.

Clinical Depression is more than just a passing case of the "blues." It is a condition which continually worsens without treatment. Patients lose interest in activities they've previously enjoyed, their sleep habits become increasingly changed, they lose their ability to mentally focus, develop feelings of worthlessness or unreasonable guilt, become increasingly fatigued, and may either gain or lose weight.

Bi-Polar Disorder was formerly known as "manic-depressive" disorder. The patient goes thorough periods of manic behavior in which they are very happy and outgoing, taking on new projects and activities, alternating with depressive episodes that cause the patient to lose interest in activities, sleep too much, and feel worthless. Often times the wild mood swings can range from sheer joy to extreme moodiness. The timing of these episodes varies from one patient to the next.

EATING DISORDERS:
Eating disorders are not usually treated with medication, though oftentimes a patient with an eating disorder also has another mental disorder

with it. In such cases the patient may be prescribed medication to treat the other disorder. As for the eating disorder itself, that takes a whole unique regimen of treatment, depending upon which disorder he or she is suffering from.

Anorexia Nervosa is the full name of the disorder in which patients are extremely fearful of gaining weight. As a result, they eat very little and oftentimes adhere to overly rigorous exercise routines. Many also use laxatives as a means to control their weight. No matter how thin and bony they become they continue to believe that they need to lose more weight; without treatment these patients will literally starve themselves to death. Anorexia can originate from anxiety issues, depression, genetics, low self-esteem, history of being abused, or extreme pressure to maintain a certain body image. Sufferers often do not recognize that they have an eating disorder.

Treatment is on a case-by-case basis but usually includes some combination of the following: A structured eating schedule, increasing of social activities, decreasing of exercise, group therapy, psychotherapy, cognitive therapy, family therapy, and education on healthy nutrition. Other therapeutic treatments may also be employed depending upon the patient's individual needs.

Bulimia Nervosa, commonly known simply as "bulimia", can manifest itself in different ways. A patient will gorge on food but then go on a strict fast, an extremely rigid exercise regimen, or use vomiting or laxatives to purge the food. Patients suffering with bulimia may look to be normal weight, so it can sometimes be more difficult to identify compared to anorexia nervosa. Bulimia comes with all sorts of dangerous side effects, such as stomach ulcers, rupture of the esophagus, and heart arrhythmias (irregular heartbeats). Bulimia can originate from depression, history of abuse, or substance abuse.

Treatment is on a case-by-case basis but usually includes some combination of the following, similar to treatment for anorexia: Psychological counseling, nutritional counseling, family therapy, and cognitive therapy. Other therapies may also be tried depending upon the patient's individual need.

Pica is when a patient eats items that are not a nutritive food source: Clay, chalk, sand, glue, paint chips, etc. True pica occurs when the behavior lasts for more than a month in a patient who is at an age when such eating is not appropriate. (Ergo, babies and toddlers would not be diagnosed with pica). Pica in and of itself is not an automatic indicator of mental illness, as many times it can be brought on by other medical conditions such as malnutrition, parasitic infections, anemia, intestinal blockage, hormonal issues, or possibly something else.

This means that in order to properly treat the condition the doctor first needs to find if the patient is suffering from other medical conditions. Therefore, a patient should expect to be scheduled for lab tests and perhaps even x-rays or barium tests to rule out certain medical conditions.

If no other medical condition is discovered, the patient will be treated psychiatrically. It is not uncommon to see pica piggy-back along with OCD or schizophrenia. If OCD or schizophrenia is not the issue, treatment may include anti-depressant medications, behavioral therapies and psychotherapy. Other therapies may also be used depending upon the patient's individual need.

PSYCHOTIC DISORDERS:

In its most basic definition, "psychosis" is when a patient has trouble distinguishing between what is real and what is not.

Schizophrenia is commonly thought to be a multiple-personality disorder, but in reality it is not. Schizophrenia usually presents itself with behavioral changes, delusions[6], hallucinations[7] and a decline in social function, employment, and school function for at least six months. A patient many not have all of these symptoms, but will

---

6 A delusion is an erroneous belief resulting from the misinterpretation of perceptions or experiences. Patients maintain these beliefs even in the face of strong evidence to the contrary. For example, a patient may believe someone is removing thoughts from his head, or that he is a super genius.

7 A hallucination is a sensory perception that happens without the proper stimulus. For example, a patient may hear voices in his head, see people who don't really exist, or feel invisible people touching him.

certainly have more than one. Schizophrenia affects each person to a different degree; no two cases are alike. Some schizophrenics may be considered "weird" but harmless by people around them, while other sufferers may experience extreme delusions and hallucinations which can cause erratic and sometimes even violent behavior.

Although schizophrenia is known to begin in adolescence it also may not show up until well into adulthood. Generally speaking, the earlier it shows up, the more severe it tends to be. Men are affected more often than women.

Schizoaffective disorder occurs when a patient has a combination of schizophrenia and a mood disorder, such as depression or bi-polar disorder. This creates a special challenge as the doctor will need to find the right combination of medication and/or therapies that will successfully treat *both* issues.

Schizophreniform disorder is essentially schizophrenia symptoms that last less than six months. If the symptoms go away on their own it is highly likely that they'll return again later.

Other psychotic disorders include: Delusional disorders, disorders caused by certain medical conditions, drug-induced psychotic disorders, and others.

Of course, I've given a very brief overview at what these illness are; only a board-certified psychiatrist can make a full and proper diagnosis of a person's illness. If you do suspect a particular diagnosis though, there is no harm in asking the doctor about your suspicions.

Chapter 6
Treatments and Options

MEDICATION

Psychiatric medications are various, and each covers specific psychiatric conditions. Therefore, a medication for psychosis is not usually prescribed for depression and a medication prescribed for an anxiety disorder will not usually be prescribed for psychosis (though there are occasional exceptions to these). However, since it is not uncommon for psychiatric patients to have more than one diagnosis, it is also not uncommon for patients to be prescribed more than one medication.

At this point we'll look at the various categories of medications available for today's patients. Please note that this is not a complete listing; I strongly recommend speaking to your psychiatrist to get more information:

Anti-Psychotics

These are used primarily for patients suffering from psychosis, such as schizo-type or delusional disorders, and sometimes for bi-polar disorders – which is not a psychosis but is a mood disorder. Some of these medications include (Brand name followed by the generic in italics):

- Abilify (*Aripiprazole*)
- Zyprexa (*Olanzapine*)
- Seroquel (*Quetiapine*)
- Risperdal (*Risperidone*)
- Haldol (*Haloperidol*)
- Clozaril (*Clozapine*)
- Melleril (*Thioridazine*)

Some of the above-mentioned medications are meant for targeting mild symptoms while others are meant for targeting stronger symptoms.

Anxiety Disorders

Anxiety Disorders are common, especially with those who have high-stress lives or have endured a traumatic or terrifying experience.

- Xanax (*Alprazolam*)
- Librium (*Chlordiazepoxide*)
- Valium (*Diazepam*)
- Klonopin (*Clonazepam*)
- BuSpar (*Busprirone*)
- Ativan (*Lorazepam*)
- Atarax (*Hydroxyzine*)

Mood Disorders:

Mood disorders oftentimes piggy back with anxiety disorders, though not always. Medications that help stabilize mood disorders include:

- Wellbutrin (*Bupropion*)
- Celexa (*Citalopram*)
- Lexapro (*Escitalopram*)
- Prozac (*Fluoxetine*)
- Paxil (*Paroxetine*)
- Zoloft (*Sertraline*)
- Sinequan (*Doxepin*)

Eating Disorders:
There isn't a medication which reverses eating disorders, however it is common for patients with eating disorders to need medication to reverse depression, anxiety, or other mental disorders. Ergo, such patients may be treated with the appropriate medications while receiving other treatments for the eating disorder.

Although all human bodies are made to function in the same basic manner, individual variances from person to person can cause medications to have different effects from person to person. These differences stem from many sources: Genetic heritage, allergies, physical health issues, use of other medications, and differences in each individual's metabolism all contribute to the problem. Because there is no "one size fits all" solution there are many different medications available in order to help as many people as possible.

It is important to know that medicinal help takes patience on your part. To begin with, many medications need to be taken regularly for at least a *few weeks,* if not longer, before full effect can be apparent. And then, if the medication is not working for some reason, the patient cannot suddenly stop taking it – he or she must be weaned off of it in order to avoid potential health effects that would be caused by suddenly stopping. After that a new medication will be tried, again taking a few weeks for full effects, and then weaned off again if that one doesn't work. Remember, no two people are alike, and their bodies will react differently to medications. On top of that, there may be instances in which your spouse has more than one diagnosis and thus needs more than one medication, further complicating the process. Do not be discouraged during this time; as I mentioned earlier, it is not uncommon to take six to twelve months to find the right medication (or combination of medications) that meets your spouse's needs.

COGNITIVE ENHANCEMENT THERAPY[8]

Cognitive Enhancement Therapy, a.k.a. CET, is an outpatient treatment program for schizophrenic and schizoaffective patients. It is a rehabilitation training program designed to restore the mental processes of perception, memory, judgment,

---

8   Endorsed by **NREPP** (**N**ational **R**egistry of **E**vidence-based **P**rograms and **P**ractices) and **SAMHSA** (**S**ubstance **A**buse and **M**ental **H**ealth **S**ervices **A**dministration)

reasoning, and socialization. Prime candidates for this treatment are those who have been stabilized, are on anti-psychotic medication, and are not abusing drugs or alcohol. The treatment usually takes about eighteen months and includes a variety of training exercises in specific succession during that time period. During this time the patient will interact with other patients, may be assigned "homework" at times, and receive coaching from the clinicians. The clinicians have master's degrees and at least two years of experience in the treatment of schizophrenic patients.

If your spouse suffers from a schizo-type disorder I recommend that you discuss this treatment with your psychiatrist.

PSYCHOSOCIAL TREATMENTS

Psychosocial treatments include psychotherapy ("talk therapy"), social and vocational training. Psychosocial treatments help diminish the negative effects of the patient's illness and strengthens the patient's well-being. This translates into fewer hospitalizations and fewer problems at home/work/school, etc. Psychosocial treatments include (but are not limited to):

- Individual talk therapy
- Psychoeducation (educating the patient and family about the illness along with coping strategies)
- Self-help and support groups

- Cognitive and behavioral therapy (focusing on the relationship between the patient's thoughts, feelings, and behavior)
- Exposure therapy (The patient is deliberately exposed to "triggers" in a controlled setting and taught techniques on how to successfully deal with the triggers)

Because each patient is his or her own unique case the psychosocial treatments used will vary according to the individual's needs. Professionals who can offer psychosocial treatments include: Psychiatrists, psychologists, psychiatric nurses, social workers, and counselors.

ELECTRO-CONVULSIVE THERAPY

This is commonly known as "Electro-shock therapy, " a.k.a. ECT. Although it has a certain social stigma attached to it, ECT is generally considered to be a safe method of treatment that is extremely helpful when other treatments aren't effective for a patient. What happens in ECT?

Basically, the patient is first given general anesthesia in order to let him or her "sleep" through the procedure. During the procedure a controlled electrical current is passed through the patient's brain with the intent of triggering a brief seizure. Because of the anesthesia the seizure will not be violent. The electrical current causes immediate changes in the patient's brain chemistry that rapidly reverses the patient's symptoms. ECT gained a bad reputation in it's early days because medical staff didn't use anesthesia or low enough doses of electricity, resulting in serious side effects such as memory loss and broken bones. Today, though, the process has been much more refined, eliminating the risk of those serious side effects.

ECT is usually employed in the following circumstances:

- Severe depression resulting in detachment from reality (known as "psychotic depression") which does not respond to other treatment.
- Severe mania, which is an extreme state of hyper-excitement and risk-taking which puts the patient or others in danger.
- Catatonia; a state in which the patient enters into long periods of motionlessness and stupor, possibly alternating with excitement and confusion.

Before receiving ECT a patient must be evaluated to be sure the treatment is appropriate. This usually includes the following:

- A complete medical history of the patient should be taken.
- A complete physical exam should be done.
- A psychiatric assessment should be done.
- Certain blood tests are needed.
- An electrocardiogram ("EKG") to ensure the patient's heart can support the rigor and physical stress of the procedure.

An ECT procedure takes less than 15 minutes to complete, with prep time and recovery time added to that. Because the patient will have general anesthesia he or she will probably need to go without food or drink for several hours before the treatment (to reduce the risk of vomiting). The patient will also undergo an exam of his or her heart and lungs. An IV will be inserted into the patient in order to administer anesthesia and a muscle relaxer. Also, a nurse will place electrode pads on the patient's head; placement of the electrodes will depend on the specific ECT method to be performed. The patient may also be given an oxygen mask. Throughout the procedure the patient's vital signs will be continually monitored to ensure health and safety. After the procedure the patient will likely feel very drowsy for a while due to the general anesthesia. He or she shouldn't be allowed to drive for several hours after the procedure.

Individual response to the treatment will vary. Some patients notice improvement within a few days, some will take a few months. No two cases are the same, therefore you cannot expect results based on someone else's case.

TRANSCRANIAL MAGNETIC STIMULATION
Transcranial Magnetic Stimulation ("TMS") is used for treating depression. It works by using magnetic fields which stimulate brain cells to release neurotransmitters in order to restore the

chemical balance in the brain. It is used for patients who have not had successful results with other therapies.

This therapy is less invasive than ECT and does not cause memory loss. It can be used on women who are breastfeeding or suffering from post-partum depression. It is also considered to be safe for children to receive.

The basic procedure is as follows: A magnetic coil is placed over the patient's head and delivers magnetic pulse energy to the patient's brain. It is similar to having an MRI[9] scan. The procedure takes about thirty minutes, is painless, and takes several sessions to achieve full results.

Check with your health insurance company to see if this therapy is covered under your plan.

VAGUS NERVE STIMULATION

The vagus nerve is a major nerve that starts in the brain stem (at the back of the base of the skull) which forks, right and left, all the way down to the abdomen. Vagus nerve stimulation uses a pace-maker-like device to deliver small doses of electrical stimulation to the vagus nerve, thereby alleviating depression.

This treatment commonly takes anywhere from several weeks to a few months to feel full effect, and is primarily for patients who have not had sufficient results from other forms of treatment. If

---

9   MRI = **M**agnetic **R**esonance **I**maging. A procedure using a magnetic field and radio waves to make pictures of internal organs and other parts of the body. This procedure does not use dangerous forms of radiation.

the patient needs a change in electrical "dose" the doctor can tweak the impulses as needed using a specialized magnetic wand in his or her office. The device is set to deliver stimulation at regular intervals and it can be switched off with a special magnet.

Although vagus nerve stimulation is safe and effective, there are some cautions to consider: First, the risks of implanting the device are the same risks as with any other surgery. After implantation the device may interfere with mammograms and thus the patient may require special positioning to get a good image. You must also know that the use of a defibrillator on the patient will damage the device, requiring a doctor's visit to replace it (of course, this is no reason to hesitate using an AED[10] if necessary!). Ultrasound[11] imaging can also damage the device, and special precautions must be employed before getting an MRI scan in order to protect the device.

A patient using vagus nerve stimulation may also require other treatments to remain mentally healthy.

ALTERNATIVE TREATMENTS

There is also a number of clinicians who believe that psychiatric illnesses are best treated

---

10 AED = **A**utomated **E**xternal **D**ifibrillator. A portable machine that is used for restoring normal heart rhythm. The machine has simple audio and visual commands which make it simple for anyone to use. It is available in many public buildings as well as ambulances.

11 Ultrasound imaging uses high frequency sound waves which can ruin the device.

without any drugs or brain stimulation. Alternative treatments include the following:

- Empathic Therapy
- Holistic Psychiatry
- Animal Assisted Therapy

Empathic therapy is founded on the concept that love, caring, and empathy are at the heart of healing. It focuses on the patient's individuality and identity while encouraging him or her to grow in self-appreciation as well as the ability to respect, love, and empathize with others.

Holistic psychiatry takes into account the patient's physical, psychiatric, and spiritual needs all in one package. It avoids (but does not necessarily denounce) the use of medications and brain stimulation techniques. It uses various diagnostic methods such as conventional testing, lab work, detoxification, nutrition, nutritional supplements, and the restoration of the nervous system. In some cases practitioners may also use alternative treatments such as acupuncture, accupressure, or herbal preparations.

Animal assisted therapy ("AAT") encourages the interaction of patients with birds, dogs, cats, and other domestic animals. The purpose of AAT is to strengthen a patient's social, emotional, or cognitive functioning. AAT has been proven to significantly reduce various symptoms related to mood, anxiety, and psychosis disorders.

It is my humble opinion that treatment for any psychiatric patient does not have to be an "either, or" situation. Each patient is a unique case and therefore each may benefit from a combination of therapies depending upon the patient's individual needs.

I strongly urge you to educate yourself on the various treatments that may apply to your spouse's situation. Do not be afraid to speak to different doctors, practitioners and clinicians. And, if you realize that a specific therapy isn't working for your spouse be sure to speak up and say something – it is not rude if you do it respectfully. You must be your spouse's advocate until he or she is stabilized because, until then, your spouse is unable to think clearly enough to advocate for him or herself. This is one of the reasons why it's so incredibly important that you accompany your spouse to *all* appointments: The professionals do not have the daily contact with your spouse like you do, your input is extremely valuable in helping them determine the best course of action for your spouse, and whether treatment options need to be changed.

And the last thing I must add is this: Psychiatric professionals tend to be conscientious and want the best for their patients, *but that doesn't make any one of them perfect*. If you truly feel in your heart that one of them is not truly helping your spouse, there is no shame in seeking another one (whether it be a psychiatrist, clinician, counselor, etc.).

Of course, there is this caution: Do not jump from one professional to another unless you find it absolutely necessary, and only after you have *FIRST* respectfully spoken with the doctor or clinician to explain your concerns so that they fully know what your concerns are *and* they are given ample opportunity to rectify the issue. Changing psychiatric professionals will interrupt your spouse's treatment because successful treatment requires the building of a sense of trust with the person treating your spouse. Each time a new doctor or clinician is sought out, that essential patient–doctor relationship has to start from scratch. Although patient records can be transferred from doctor to doctor, these files can only tell a part of the story because of the uniqueness of every case and patient.

Chapter 7
Support for Yourself and Your Children

Caring for your mentally ill spouse can seem very challenging sometimes. Depending upon your spouse's diagnosis and treatment you may find it time consuming, frustrating, discouraging, and even overwhelming at times. In spite of your best efforts and best intentions, supporting your spouse can take a toll on *you*. Don't let yourself drown in the wake of the challenges; there are many support groups and community helps for those who are helping family members who are mentally ill.

If you are fortunate enough to have a network of supportive friends and family members then I strongly urge you to lean on them as you journey through this challenging period. Don't expect them to have all the "answers", but don't discard them as a valuable resource for you. Schedule get-togethers with your family and friends on a regular basis, at least once a week if not more. Be sure to include your children in these weekly gatherings, they need the stability as much as you do.

Also, if you are a person of faith, I strongly encourage you to schedule a session with your trusted spiritual leaders to discuss your family situation. Your faith leaders and congregation members can be such a blessing for you and your children. Often times places of worship have children and youth groups that can benefit your kids, and adult groups that can benefit you. Some may even offer support groups as well; it's worth looking into. It is also worth remembering that, in many denominations, the congregational leaders may have some education in social work and psychology, making them a valuable resource to help you spiritually as well as emotionally as you go through this journey.

Aside from family, friends, and your faith, you should also look into your community's offerings of support groups and meetings. Mental health clinics, social workers, psychiatric hospitals, and regular hospitals – especially those with behavioral or psychiatric units – should have plenty of information for you. You may also want to look into local charities who help the homeless; many psychiatric patients become homeless, thus such charities are familiar with local mental health support networks. If your closest local groups are still too far away for you to attend, there are also online groups and meetings you can join: Simply search the Internet for "*mental illness support group online*" and the computer will give you pages of links to explore.

You can try any combination of these suggestions and see what's right for you and your children. Whether you try one thing or many, be sure you get out and build your support network, and get the help your kids need as well. Do not let yourself or your family stagnate during this time.

Chapter 8
The Obstacles You Will Encounter

No matter how dedicated you are to your sick spouse, you will encounter serious situations that threaten to derail you if you are not careful. This chapter will discuss some of these situations.

INFIDELITY

This is the BIG one, so I'm going to tackle it first: No matter how dedicated and supportive you are of your sick spouse, the temptation of a potential lover can rear its ugly head during this period of time. This is understandable: The Potential Lover ("PL") is usually a person who seems to be what you *wish* your spouse would be, *or* is similar to the person whom your spouse was before he or she became sick. The PL is probably someone who is easy to talk to and confide in, creating a sense of camaraderie. You may catch yourself finding reasons to talk to or hang out with the PL, and before you know it your emotions are stepping into dangerous territory. It's even *more* dangerous if the PL has developed mutual feelings towards you. Know this: Any extramarital affair, whether emotional or sexual[12], *will* derail your spouse's recovery. How can that be? It's all too easy:

---

12 An emotional affair is a romantic affair in which no sexual activity takes place. In contrast, a sexual affair includes sexual activity.

First of all, the acceptance of an extramarital lover, whether emotional or sexual, only serves to divide your priorities. The lover takes up space in your mind, becoming a separate set of thoughts and plans which distract you from helping your spouse get well again. Although you may try to convince yourself that you can keep both relationships, you really can't without sacrificing your spouse. It is a fact that when a married person takes a lover the married person becomes more critical of his or her own spouse. You will start to focus more on your spouse's negative behaviors instead of the positive progress your spouse is making – it is the rationale that enables you to continue seeing the lover. This, in turn, erodes at your marriage, slowly strangling the repair of your relationship with your spouse.

You cannot properly advocate for your spouse and his or her treatment when your mind becomes divided like that. This is the time in your marriage when your spouse needs you the most; it is what you signed up for when you vowed to stay together through "better or worse, in sickness and in health, forsaking all others" and "keep yourself only unto" him or her. Your spouse needs *you*, the avowed life mate, to be his or her stronghold during the process of diagnosis and treatment. Yes, this can be challenging, but your spouse is *sick*, and cannot do it him or herself; this is *not* the time to wimp out. Although you will need some time to blow off some steam and have some crazy fun once in a while, taking a lover is *never* an acceptable way to do this. It's better to go blow off steam with friends and family instead.

Aside from all of that, the discovery of the affair would have devastating effects on your children and your sick spouse. Your children will feel confused, anxious, and maybe even angry at you for betraying the other parent. They will always harbor the memories of what it did to the family *AND* it teaches them that it's acceptable to bail out on the people you love. That is *not* a life lesson that you need to teach your kids. As for the sick spouse, he or she doesn't need to have that emotional devastation inflicted in the midst of overcoming mental illness. It will completely derail any stability your spouse has achieved, pushing him or her right back to the bottom again. Once you've destroyed your spouse's trust in you it'll be extremely difficult to continue treatment with the spouse's full cooperation. In many cases, the discovery of an affair causes the sick spouse to begin believing you are trying to get rid of him or her, and paranoia can set in. Yes, you can do a whole lot of damage to your kids and your spouse when the affair is discovered.

I know it isn't easy to turn down a tempting PL. You may be feeling overwhelmed, and even be angry with your spouse for being sick – which doesn't make sense, but it happens.

Remember, your spouse didn't choose to get sick any more than a person chooses to get brain cancer. If you are having a tough time working through your emotions during this time period I strongly suggest that you speak to others in your support groups, your spouse's psychiatrist, or any other professional regularly involved in your spouse's treatment and care. Your emotions are normal and valid, and you aren't the first one to have these thoughts and feelings. You aren't evil for having them, but you also don't need to destroy your spouse and your family because of them. You have control over your actions – and it's best to control them in a way that doesn't destroy trust and integrity.

Speaking from personal experience, I myself had to contend with such a temptation during the period before my husband received his diagnosis, when he was at his worst:

The PL was one of my co-workers, and as he was going through a separation from his wife we connected over our difficult marital situations. As I got to know him I found that he was a lot like my husband was before he became sick: In a nutshell, he was a hard worker, a very involved dad, a compassionate person, and a generous soul who liked outdoorsy activities. Gosh I missed those things in my husband, terribly! The PL and I started making play-dates with our younger kids and became close friends. I didn't worry about my feelings for the PL until he made it known that his own feelings for me were growing. *That's* when I had to do a lot of soul searching, and it wasn't easy: I had to face some very uncomfortable truths, and I had to force myself to think of what the future could hold. I knew that "staying in the moment" wasn't an option – any daydream I dreamed wasn't going to have a happy ending in real life. As much as I wanted an "easy out" from my troubles and responsibilities, I knew I had to make the painful decision to drop my friendship with the PL before we went too far – and in my case it required that I quit my job. It was *not* easy to walk away from him – he was what I was missing in my husband and it was one of the toughest decisions I'd made in a very long time. So yeah, I totally understand the draw of a PL when your life seems to have gone to hell, and I totally understand how hard it is to do the right thing.

Did I really make the right decision? You bet! When my husband's treatment started taking full effect I saw the dark, brooding, paranoid stranger begin to fade away and my normal, rational, beautiful husband started coming back – even though it took a little time, it was well worth fighting for!

FAMILY REJECTION

Do not be surprised if some members of your family deny your spouse's sickness. Realize that they aren't trying to be mean or difficult; a diagnosis of mental illness is very tough news and some simply won't want to accept it. As I've mentioned earlier in this book, this can be manifest in different ways: Perhaps some choose to remain in denial that your spouse has a psychiatric diagnosis, thinking that it's "just a phase." Others will deny anything, even "a phase." Maybe some family members will accept it, but then blame *you* for it. Perhaps some may even claim that you are lying about it for some ulterior motive. Or, possibly, they accept it and then have nothing more to do with you or your spouse. You may even have a family member who will seem accepting and sympathetic to your face but then be the complete opposite behind your back. You can never predict how people will react to such news.

In our case we had a combination of such ones, which is to be expected I suppose. Although most of our family members took the situation in stride not all of them were so good about it. There was one who insisted I was just trying to get attention by "trying to make us think he's crazy!" A few other ones simply acted like I didn't exist. One decided that me and my husband simply needed some time apart for a while and that would fix everything. Another one decided that we should get a divorce. One member was noncommittal but at least she always listened when I needed someone to talk to.

It is a very difficult thing to have to deal with negative family members: You already have your hands full helping your spouse, caring for your children, keeping your employment, and juggling the myriad other daily duties that come up. Adding negative family members only adds to the headache, I know. You are not in the wrong if you choose to politely avoid the negative ones. Their negativity is *their* problem, not yours.

Whatever it is, don't let their reactions keep you down. Don't forget that your spouse's psychiatrist – a board-certified medical doctor – performed a comprehensive evaluation on your spouse: The diagnosis is *real*, and it is nobody's fault. Your spouse needs proper treatment no matter what others try to say about it. You need to do what is best for your *spouse* because your spouse is not well enough to seek treatment on his or her own. It is a tragedy when you have family members who are not supportive, but giving in to *their* pressure will only serve to hurt your spouse.

DEPRESSION AND ANXIETY

Staying with a diagnosed spouse can be very emotionally draining during the diagnosis and initial treatment period. As I've already mentioned, while you're trying to be supportive of your spouse you still need to maintain your employment, your home, your children, various appointments, and so on. At this point you are the entire backbone of your family unit while waiting for your spouse's treatment to take full effect. Indeed, it is a challenge – even more so if you don't have full family support to back you up. Although not every spouse of a mentally ill mate develops depression or anxiety, there are many who do. It is an individual situation that cannot be predicted. For this reason you shouldn't be ashamed if you find yourself going into depression or anxiety. The load you are carrying can seem large, and it's not a surprise if you feel the pressure. Stress like this can affect your own brain chemistry, and there is no shame in seeking help for yourself in the beginning stages if you must. Do not be in denial of your own needs if you feel yourself slipping.

Common symptoms of depression include (but are not limited to):

- Difficulties in concentration
- Lack of energy, fatigue
- Feeling hopeless, guilty, or worthless
- Sleep issues such as: Insomnia, excessive sleepiness, or frequently interrupted sleep.
- Restlessness
- Appetite issues: Either overeating or loss of appetite.
- Loss of interest in usual activities or hobbies.
- Headaches, aches, pains, cramps, etc. that are not easily remedied with treatment.
- Continual sad, anxious, or empty feelings.

Common symptoms of anxiety include (but are not limited to):

- Feeling apprehensive or powerless.
- Having a sense of impending doom.
- Increased heart rate or breathing

- Increased sweating or trembling
- Feeling weakness or tiredness

Of course, it is normal to have one or two symptoms when initially faced with a spouse's mental illness: Who can eat or sleep with *that* kind of news?! Who wouldn't feel apprehensive in the beginning?! But, if the symptoms continue, get worse, or start adding on, you need to seriously consider the possibility that you may be experiencing depression and/or anxiety. It does not mark you as a weak person if you develop depression or anxiety, it only means that you are human.

Why would one well spouse develop these conditions while another one doesn't? There are no easy answers to that question. There are so many variables because each couple's situation is different: Each spouse is a unique person who has his or her unique combination of physical metabolism, mental chemistry, family dynamic, cultural influence and lifestyle – no single situation is the exact same as another's. Therefore, nobody has the right to judge anyone else on the matter. In this case, a judgmental attitude is nothing more than a case of ignorance, so don't take it to heart – they don't know what they're talking about.

How can you reduce the possibility that you may develop depression or anxiety? I suppose I can't say this enough: Attend support groups and meetings on a regular basis – preferably in person, but if that's impossible then at least do it online. Go to more than one if you feel you need it. Combine in-person and Internet meetings if you need it. It is also important that you also confide in the psychiatrist and other professionals involved in your spouse's treatment; they are there to support you as well as your spouse. If you are fortunate enough to have family members and friends to lean on, don't be afraid to do so. They love you and want to be there for you, even if they don't have all the "answers."

The basic idea is that you must not hide yourself away from the world. You aren't the only spouse learning how to navigate your mate's illness, and you don't have to be the only one dealing with it. This is exactly why there are support groups, meetings, family, and friends.

Chapter 9
Possible Setbacks

Although setbacks are *not* inevitable, it is better to be prepared for the possibility of encountering them rather than be caught by surprise. This chapter will discuss some of the setbacks that you may be challenged with. Please note that the information in this chapter is only generalized; it is not exhaustive. Therefore I strongly recommend that you schedule a thorough discussion about these topics with your spouse's psychiatrist.

SIDE EFFECTS

One of the most common issues is the occurrence of side effects resulting from treatment. Not everyone experiences side effects, and those who do will experience them at varying degrees depending upon the individual. In some cases side effects are only temporary, and in other cases they continue for as long as the treatment continues. In cases where side effects do appear they are usually manifest at a tolerable level. In some cases, though, side effects may be strong enough so that the patient discontinues the treatment.

Of course, not everyone experiences side effects, and an even lesser number of people experience life threatening side effects. Do not let fear of side effects prevent you from getting your spouse the treatment he or she really needs. Trust your doctor, and keep yourself educated.

That being said, let's discuss the most common side effects associated with various psychiatric treatments:

Anti-depression medications come in a variety of classes, and each class has it's own known side effects. Some of these medications can cause sexual dysfunction, i.e. extreme hindrance of sexual pleasure in both male and female patients. Although this isn't a physically dangerous kind of side effect it can still cause a patient to discontinue use of the medication. Fortunately, this side effect is normally associated with only certain classes of medications, meaning that not all anti-depressants have this side effect. A patient may be able to request a prescription from a different class of anti-depressants in order to alleviate this problem. If the patient must stay on the medication there are still strategies to lessen sexual dysfuntion – but never employ these without your doctor's supervision. Such strategies include (but are not limited to): Lowering the therapeutic dose, adding another medication to the prescription, and timing sexual activity to when the body's drug level is low. Be aware of two things though:

1. Changes in medication may take a few weeks before noticeable improvement takes place.

2. Changes in medication in itself may cause side effects.

73

Aside from sexual issues, other side effects of Anti-depressants may include: Insomnia, nausea, agitation, nervousness, blurred vision, seizures, constipation, bladder problems, drowsiness and dry mouth, depending upon the medication being taken. These are just the lighter side effects.

Some side effects can actually be life threatening. For example, medications in the SSRI[13] class may cause *Serotonin Syndrome*, symptoms of which include fever, confusion, muscle stiffness, and problems with one's vital organs. For patients taking medication in the MAOI[14] class, they must be sure to avoid any foods or medications that contain the amino acid *tyramine* for it can cause a sharp rise in blood pressure leading to a stroke. Such foods and medications include: Decongestant medications, fish, cheese, chocolate, soy sauce, processed foods, pickles, and alcohol. Patients taking medications in the SNRI[15] class may experience symptoms of liver failure, a.k.a. *Jaundice*, which are: Yellowing of skin and eyes, nausea, loss of appetite, and unusually dark urine.

Anti-psychotic medications are normally classed as either *typical*, or *atypical*. Typical anti-psychotics are first-generation medications that are sub-classed as low, medium, and high potency. These medications are used in cases of psychosis

13 SSRI = Selective Serotonin Reuptake Inhibitors
14 MAOI = Monoamine Oxidase Inhibitors
15 SNRI = Serotonin/Norepinephrine Reuptake Inhibitors

and agitation. Atypical medications are second-generation medications and are generally used for depression, bi-polar disorders, and psychosis. The side effects of atypical medications tend to be less severe than those of typical medications. Atypical medications also tend to be less addictive and have stronger efficacy. Typical medications, however, tend to stay in the system longer, thus reducing the chance of relapse into psychosis. Although atypical medications are preferred, there may be cases in which the typical medications may be more appropriate for the patient, depending upon the individual's circumstances and tolerance for medications.

Side effects of typical anti-psychotics may include: Urinary retention (inability to fully urinate), lactation (even in men), low blood pressure when changing position, drowsiness, weight gain, constipation, and irregular menstrual periods, among others.

Side effects of atypical anti-psychotics may include: Weight gain, onset of type-2 Diabetes, increase in blood cholesterol levels, heart rhythm issues, serious infections of the heart, and sexual dysfunction, among others.

Side effects that span both typical and atypical medications include:

- *Tardive dykinesia*: Uncontrollable movements of the mouth, head, torso, or arms. It can manifest itself even after long time use of the medication. Because of this, dosages should be kept as low as therapeutically possible.

- *Akathisia*: Persistent feeling of restlessness in the muscles so that the patient feels the continual need to move. This may be alleviated by adding beta blocker or benzodiazapine medications to the patient's treatment plan.
- *Low white blood cell count*: This puts this patient at a higher risk of contracting infections, and is usually seen in 3 percent of patients taking the atypical medication called Clozapine.
- *Neuroleptic Malignant Syndrome*: This is a deadly side effect that is known by a high fever, confusion, and muscular stiffness. The patient must be taken to the emergency room immediately, as this deadly disorder has the potential to induce coma or delirium lasting for several weeks.

Anti-anxiety medications are various and have side effects that include: Nausea, dizziness, confusion, drowsiness, nightmares, headaches, bowel problems, insomnia, nervousness and others, depending upon which medication the patient is taking.

Transcranial Magnetic Stimulation is, according to the Mayo Clinic, the least invasive of the brain stimulating procedures used in treating depression. However, this does not mean it is without side effects. The side effects may include:

Headache, lightheadedness, and the twitching of facial muscles. Less common side effects include seizures or mania (especially in bi-polar patients).

Electroconvulsive Therapy is performed under general anesthesia, as stated in chapter 6 of this book. Although it is a safe and effective treatment, there still may be side effects, such as: Temporary confusion, memory loss, nausea, muscle aches, and jaw pain. Also, if your spouse is a heart patient you may want to be sure the doctor is aware of this before getting ECT treatment, as certain heart conditions can be aggravated by the treatment.

Vagus Nerve Stimulation is safe but there are some side effects to be aware of. Side effects which happen during the half-minute the device is on include: Hoarseness, cough, and shortness of breath. Other side effects can include voice changes, sore throat, headaches, difficulty in swallowing, and nausea, among others.

If your spouse show signs of side effects with any treatments you should inform the doctors and clinicians, even if the side effects are mild. It is important for the professionals to be informed and updated in order to give your spouse the best care possible. You spouse may not have to put up with side effects, even mild ones, if there is an effective treatment that may give him or her no side effects at all.

RELAPSE

A relapse is when your spouse becomes ill again after having achieved his or her recovery. Often times the patient does not recognize that he or she is slipping back into the sickness. There are three main causes for relapse:

Dosage weakness: The current treatment may not be strong enough for therapeutic effect. For example, the medication dosage may need to be strengthened, or the vagus nerve stimulator may need to be tweaked. In some cases it may be that the medication must be changed altogether, or perhaps another treatment needs to be added along with the current treatment.

Side effects: As discussed, side effects can sometimes become so uncomfortable that the patient refuses to continue the treatment. It is best if the patient speaks up about this, but many times they won't for various reasons. Perhaps he or she doesn't want to burden you with complaints. Or perhaps he or she doesn't want to be perceived as difficult, or a "whiner baby." Perhaps he or she is afraid of being perceived as weak or incapable. Whatever the reason, it is important for the well spouse to monitor the sick spouse's use of the treatment, especially in treatments involving medication: Ensure that your spouse is taking the medicine *and* ensure that he or she is taking the correct dose. If your spouse begins to slack off on treatment, it is time to investigate the possibility of adverse side effects that may not have been voiced.

Speak with your spouse *and* the clinicians involved in your spouse's treatments. Just be aware that making changes in treatment plans can take several months of tweaking before finding the right thing that works specifically for your spouse.

Noncompliance with treatment. Sometimes, when a patient is feeling healthy and stable the patient will recognize that he or she has become a healthy, rational, contributing person to the family and to the community. He or she feels strong, resilient, and mentally balanced. These, of course, are good things, but sometimes such ones decide they are completely cured at this point and no longer need treatment. As a result, they fail to continue refilling their prescriptions and/or stop making new appointments for other treatments. Usually, the patient does not inform his or her spouse about these things, and so the well spouse is initially unaware of it. Granted, in some cases a person can go off his or her treatment and remain well afterward, but this isn't always the case. As a result, the patient begins showing symptoms of slipping back into sickness again, but the patient, being the sick one, doesn't realize that he or she is getting sick again. Sometimes this can happen quickly, and other times it may take several months to show symptoms again. Regardless of how long it takes for onset of symptoms, it is usually the well spouse who eventually begins to notice that something is "not right" with the patient.

Sometimes it isn't a willful action of the patient. Perhaps the patient *meant* to get around to refilling the prescription or making another appointment, but never actually got around to it. And the longer he or she doesn't get around to it, the more he or she begins to think that "I'm doing okay so far, maybe I don't need this treatment anymore after all." Of course, it still ends up with the same result: The patient starts showing signs of getting sick again but doesn't realize it.

Please don't be discouraged if your spouse relapses. Yes, it will be maddening when you realize he or she has kept side effects from you or stopped the treatments, but getting angry does not fix the problem. Instead, the first thing you should do, if your spouse is able, is to ask your spouse if he or she is still taking the treatments as recommended, and if not, why did he or she stop. This will give you a clue as to whether dosage, side effects, or non-compliance is the issue. After you've discussed this with your spouse you must call the treating psychiatrist and discuss the relapse with him or her. Be aware that the psychiatrist will want to know what symptoms are being observed, how long the patient has gone without treatment, and what (if you know) caused the patient to discontinue the treatments.

Chapter 10
Famous Mentally Ill People

Still feel a sense of stigma for having a spouse who has been diagnosed with a mental illness? Let me ease your mind: People diagnosed with mental illnesses can be restored and live full, productive lives as members of the community with proper medical care and treatment. To give you an idea of how doable this is, let me give you a list of famous people who have have made great contributions in spite of their mental illness. Of course, this is not a complete listing:

Vivien Leigh:
Actress whose notable work was in "*Gone With the Wind*". Diagnosed with cyclical bi-polar disorder with hallucinations.

John Nash:
Genius mathematician who earned the Nobel Prize in economics in 1994. Diagnosed with paranoid schizophrenia.

Connie Francis:
Singer and actress, diagnosed with bi-polar disorder.

Richard Simmons:
Famous diet-and-exercise guru. Battled with

anorexia and bulimia for many of his younger years.

Brooke Shields:
Actress; Suffered a severe episode of post-partum depression after the birth of her baby.

Judy Collins:
Singer and songwriter; battled with bulimia in the 1970s.

Buzz Aldrin:
Well-known astronaut, diagnosed with bi-polar disorder.

Vaslov Nijinsky:
Russian dancer, diagnosed with schizophrenia.

Tom Harrell:
Highly respected jazz musician. Diagnosed with schizophrenia.

Margot Kidder:
Actress; diagnosed with schizophrenia in her early 20's, and then later was also diagnosed with bi-polar disorder.

Joey Ramone:
Leader of the punk rock band "The Ramones", diagnosed with schizophrenia.

Herschel Walker:
Football star diagnosed with disassociative identity disorder.

Linda Hamilton:
Movie and television actress. Diagnosed with bi-polar disorder.

Tracey Gold:
Child actress from the family sit-com "Growing Pains." Battled with anorexia nervosa in her earlier years.

Carrie Fisher:
Movie actress, now comedienne. Diagnosed with bi-polar disorder.

Andy Goram:
Scottish soccer player who was diagnosed with schizophrenia.

Robert Downey Jr. :
Movie actor. Diagnosed with bi-polar disorder.

Peter Green:
Guitarist for the music group Fleetwood Mac. Diagnosed with schizophrenia.

Robin Williams:
Actor and comedian. Diagnosed with bi-polar disorder.

Syd Barrett:
Member of the band Pink Floyd. Diagnosed with schizophrenia.

Jean-Claude Van Damme:
Movie actor and martial artist. Diagnosed with bi-polar disorder.

Jim Carrey:
Movie actor. Diagnosed with bi-polar disorder.

Peter Gabriel:
Singer and songwriter. Diagnosed with bi-polar disorder.

Brian Wilson:
Singer and songwriter. Diagnosed with bi-polar disorder.

As you can see, with proper care and treatment, patients with psychiatric illnesses can be restored to good mental health and make valuable contributions to society. It is not as hopeless or as stigmatizing as you may believe.

Chapter 11
The Worst Case Scenario

Unfortunately, not everything always comes up roses for some people. Although the vast majority of patients successfully recover after treatment, there are some tough cases in which a patient must undergo long-term treatment in an institutional setting. Yes, this can be heartbreaking – it is not on anyone's bucket list. How can you get through this kind of ordeal?

Educate Yourself:
The first thing you need to do is educate yourself, because the more you know about a situation the more control you have over the situation. Educate yourself on your spouse's illness and the treatments involved. Educate yourself on the institution's in-house visitation policies as well as home visitation policies. Be informed on what you can do if you need to contact your spouse outside of normal visiting hours. Educate yourself on what you can do if ever you disagree with a treatment or wish to transfer your spouse to a different facility. Educate yourself on what your rights are.

Know the Staff:
Get to know exactly who your spouse's doctors and clinicians will be in the institution (in many

cases a patient may be assigned a different set of doctors and clinicians when institutionalized). Know who the charge nurses are on each shift and who the floor manager is. Stay in regular contact with them; this lessens the likelihood of misunderstandings and mistakes, and it keeps you informed of changes, ensuring your spouse is receiving the best care to fit his or her needs. Also, don't neglect to get to know the aides who care for your spouse. It is also important to get to know the facility's dietician and the nutritionist, as this ensures that if your spouse has special dietary needs they will be properly met. It is a fact that patients who have very involved family members tend to receive more accurate care because misunderstandings and human errors are caught early and taken care of.

Know the Facility:
Educate yourself on the facility's rating and history. Does it have a low incidence of medical mistakes? Is the staff properly licensed and trained? Is there any history of patient neglect or abuse? What are the plans for keeping patients safe and protected? Does the facility look clean and in good repair? What security measures are in place? What are the policies for handling a difficult patient? Does the facility have recreational or educational programs? If so, how are the programs supervised? Do the staff members seem warm and friendly?

Keep lists:

Be sure you keep a list of your spouse's doctors and clinicians along with their contact numbers. Be sure your list includes contact numbers for the main facility, your spouse's psychiatrist and/ or psychologist, the designated pharmacy, and the number for the particular floor or section that your spouse is assigned to. Ensure that all of *your* personal contact information is available to them as well. You should also keep a list of all of your spouse's medications, dosages, and frequency of use, and keep the list up-to-date; you never know when you'll need that information.

Know Your Spouse's Rights:

Even though your spouse is an institutionalized patient, your spouse still has rights that cannot be taken from him or her. Because patient rights is an involved topic I have dedicated the entirety of the next chapter to this subject.

Chapter 12
Patient's Rights

This is a listing of a patient's rights, whether they are institutionalized or being treated on an outpatient basis. Although the vast majority of psychiatric facilities are good quality health care institutions, it doesn't hurt to take notice that your spouse's rights are being respected:

- Patients have the right to receive and keep a copy of their rights on paper.
- Institutionalization is not grounds for depriving a patient of his or her civil rights. Therefore, patients retain the right to vote and maintain any certifications or licenses they've already earned.
- Competent patients have the right to refuse medication or treatment.
- Patients have the right to be fully informed about their treatments before consenting to them. Informed consent includes knowing how the treatment will be administered, prognosis of the treatment, side effects, risks, and possible consequences for refusing the treatment. (Consequences cannot include any form of punishment, coercion, negative reinforcement, or undue restrictions). Informed consent also means that the patient must be informed if the treatment is experimental.

- Patients have the right to be protected from abuse, neglect, and/or mistreatment from staff and fellow patients. Abuse can be verbal, sexual, physical, emotional, financial, or mental.
- Patients have a right to wear appropriate personal clothing. They cannot be forced to wear "hospital clothes" if they do not want to.
- They have a right to dwell in a safe, clean, secure environment.
- They have a right to a balanced, nutritious diet. Food cannot be forcibly withheld. Special diet needs must be accommodated (such as for patients with diabetes, food allergies, low salt, low cholesterol, etc.).
- They have a right to access items necessary for personal hygiene.
- They have a right to utilize personal storage space for clothing and personal items.
- They have a right to reasonable privacy in sleeping, bathing, and toileting areas.
- They have a right to receive visitors at reasonable times. They have a right to privacy during these visits.
- They have a right to freely communicate with others either inside or outside the institution.
- They have a right to receive reasonable medical and dental care.
- They have a right to receive an individualized treatment plan and the right to actively participate in that plan.
- They have a right to keep their medical care and treatment private and confidential.

- Patients cannot be *required* to work beyond maintaining their personal space and items. If work training is offered the patient must have the freedom to choose whether to participate. The patient must be informed of the nature of the work, rate of pay, length of pay period, how pay rate is determined, what deductions are taken and why.
- Patients between the ages of 5 – 21 must be allowed access to the same educational and vocational services that are offered outside the institution.
- Patients have the right to receive letters and mail unopened. If there is a limitation put on their mail they must be told why. You can reverse the limitation by appealing to the director of the institution.
- If a patient cannot read or write, the institution must provide staff that can perform the reading or writing for the patient.
- If the patient does not speak the local language the institution must make all reasonable efforts to interpret for the patient.
- Patients have the right to freedom from restraint or seclusion unless they are a danger to themselves or to others. Restraints and seclusion must not be given more than is absolutely necessary.
- Patients have a right to practice the religion of his or her choice. This includes the right to pray, worship, read religious literature and eat a diet that corresponds to their religion's rules. The facility cannot force a patient to attend

particular religious services.

- Patients who have *voluntarily* committed themselves to the institution have the right to leave at any time they wish.

These rights can be limited only through a physician's written order. The physician, however, is required to specify the justification for the limitation in the written order. For example, if it is discovered that a patient has been receiving illegal drugs in his mail (unfortunately, this does happen from time to time), then the physician could justify having that particular patient's mail opened and inspected before the patient receives it. So long as a patient is acting lawfully and is not endangering himself, other patients, staff, or visitors, the patient cannot have his or her rights limited.

Of course, in spite of all these rights the big question must be asked:

> *What if my spouse is mentally incompetent and cannot give proper consent or make valid decisions regarding his or her care?*

First of all, it is important to know that being institutionalized does **_not_** automatically denote mental incompetency. Incompetency can only be determined on a case by case basis. If your spouse is found to be incompetent the law provides for what is called "substituted consent". Substituted consent is when an authorized person is designated to give the consent and makes decisions on the patient's behalf, whether the patient is either incompetent or otherwise unable to give consent (such as a coma patient). Who is an authorized person? The person who is the patient's health care proxy or has durable power of attorney can give substituted consent. It can also be someone who is a court-appointed guardian or the patient's next of kin (depending on your state laws). If there is no appointed proxy or power of attorney the facility must initiate a court procedure in order to appoint one for the patient. *In the vast majority of cases a patient's spouse can be designated to give the substituted consent.*

If, for some reason, you decline to be the designated person, you may unwittingly be forfeiting your right to be given *any* medical information about your spouse. For example, if your spouse falls and hurts himself, the staff will likely be legally prevented from telling you about it due to the federal HIPAA[16] privacy law.

Being authorized to give substituted consent is a major reason why it's so important for you to be educated on your spouse's illness and treatments, as well as have a good rapport with the treating clinicians. If you have any questions about substituted consent I strongly recommend you discuss the topic with the psychiatrist.

---

16 Health Insurance Portability and Accountability Act. I give detailed information about this in Appendix 5 of this book.

Of course, there are some exceptions regarding the scope of substituted consent. In cases where a patient is in immediate danger of harming himself or someone else, or in an emergency situation, the staff members can legally make the decisions without obtaining consent. For example, if a patient trips and knocks himself unconscious, the staff can immediately begin treatment on the patient before getting the substituted consent for treatment. Or, if a patient suddenly flies into a violent rage the staff can legally give appropriate medication or apply restraints before getting consent. However, it is imperative that as soon as it is reasonable, the designated proxy, guardian, or person with the power of attorney – who is most likely *you* – should be contacted and be fully informed of the situation and how it was handled.

Aside from these emergency exceptions, what can you do if you truly believe that your spouse's rights are being trampled on? First, be sure you are completely informed about the situation: For example, is the staff actually *withholding* food from your spouse, or is your spouse simply *refusing* to eat the food that is set before him or her? If it is a case of refusal, ask the staff why your spouse is refusing to eat and what steps they are taking to encourage him or her to eat. You should also review the diet they are offering your spouse: Perhaps they are unwittingly offering your spouse food that he or she cannot eat. For example, a Muslim or Jewish patient may refuse all pork products on religious grounds, or a Christian patient may refuse all meat during Lent for the same reason. Or, perhaps your spouse has a food allergy and the offered foods contain the allergen. It is important to ensure that the facility's dietician, cooks, and cafeteria crew have the correct information regarding your spouse's dietary needs. In some cases, though, it may simply be a cultural difference in food preferences.

I am reminded of a time when I was helping care for a group of dementia patients. One patient was a born-and-raised Chinese national, and sometimes he would refuse to eat the food the facility offered him. Upon his refusal the staff would inform his designated family member and the family would bring in some home cooked Chinese cuisine for him to eat. Since this was a Chinese family, they always had something on hand for him. Although this meant the man would eat a little later than the other patients, at least he would still be fed, and all would be well.

Of course, issues with food is just one example of a rights issue that may be faced. If you find that it's not a matter of refusal, but that your spouse's rights have indeed been limited, ask to see the physician's order that was written for it. Ask questions about what led up to the limitations. If you are not satisfied with the answers, or if you find that no order has been written, remember that, although the vast majority of institutions are honest and caring places, sometimes you may run into a staff member who has erred in judgment. This is when you need to use the "chain of command" to place your complaints.[17]

If you know which staff member(s) made the horrendous error, take the complaint to that person's boss first. For example, if it was an aide who erred, take it to the nurse who is overseeing the aide. If it was a nurse, take the complaint to that nurse's charge nurse. If it is a charge nurse who erred, go to the floor manager. If it happened to be the floor manager who erred, then go to the director or administrator of the facility. If, instead, you aren't sure who made the mistake, take the complaint to the shift's charge nurse first. If, instead, you have an issue with someone else other than the medical staff, (such as the maintenance man, the dietitician, recreational aides, etc.) then start with the floor manager.

If the first link in the chain does not resolve the problem within a reasonable time then you should go to the next link up the chain with your complaint. It is important to realize that it's a matter of basic respect to go directly according to the chain of command; do not step on toes by skipping links in the chain if you don't need to. Not only are you wasting time when you skip links (because the higher link will simply instruct you to first go to the appropriate lower links you skipped), but you will be viewed as rude, irritating, and disrespectful if you

---

17 The basic chain of command, from bottom to top is as follows: Aide, Nurse, Charge Nurse, Floor Manager, Director of Nursing, Administrator.

skip the links. Your goal is not to be rude or disrespectful, for that only serves to make *you* a problem to be solved. Instead, your goal is to ensure that *your spouse's* problem is solved. You will achieve much better results for your spouse by being a cooperative caregiver who respects the chain of authority. By using the chain of command you are giving the facility a fair chance to rectify the situation and ensure that a similar situation does not happen again to either your spouse or another patient.

If, after you've gone through the proper channels, you still feel that your spouse is having his or her rights unfairly denied there are other options available for you to help your spouse. This will be discussed in the next chapter.

Chapter 13
Filing a Complaint

Although I'm sure you've seen the Hollywood horror stories of neglectful or abusive psychiatric institutions, the truth is that most facilities are conscientious and seek only the best care for their patients. In spite of this though, human error rears it's ugly head sometimes and missteps can happen. If you feel your spouse or another patient is being wronged, and the facility has done nothing to resolve the issue after you've properly gone through the chain of command, you need to know what you can do next.

First of all, what do I mean by "wronged"? I mean any of the following:
- Patient abuse or neglect
- Staff incompetence which compromises the safety and well-being of patients
- Staff taking advantage of patients in financial, sexual, or other ways
- Insurance fraud
- Violations of patients' rights
- Failure to protect patients from harm

If, after trying to resolve the issue with the facility's chain of command the complaint has not been properly corrected within a reasonable length of time, you will need to address the problem with your local mental health agencies who oversee your area's caregivers.

I recommend that you first start with contacting your local ombudsman. An ombudsman is a neutral party who is appointed to investigate complaints against violations of rights or improper administration. In some countries this may also be known as the Inspector General or Citizen Advocate. There is no charge for using the services of an ombudsman. All health care facilities, whether it's a nursing home, psychiatric institution or a hospital, should have freely accessible information on contacting your local ombudsman. Many facilities have their own ombudsman, and an honest, competent facility will not hinder your access to this information. If your spouse's facility is being uncooperative you can contact a different health care institution and request the information, or you can search for your local ombudsman online. Your local mental health support groups, clinics, and meeting places may also have the information you seek.

There are also many other resources available to help you, depending upon who or what your complaint is with. For example:

- If your complaint is with a particular psychiatrist, therapist, or psychologist you can file a complaint with your state's medical board or your state's board of health and mental hygiene.

- If the complaint is with only a psychiatrist you can file a complaint with the American Psychiatric Association.[18]

- If your complaint is with a therapist or psychologist (but not a psychiatrist) you may look to see if he or she is a member of the American Psychological Association or the National Association of Social Workers and lodge a complaint with them.[19]

- You may also consider contacting the Joint Commission,[20] which accredits home health agencies, nursing homes, outpatient clinics, hospitals, behavioral health care programs, and managed care programs, among others. They investigate complaints of patient care, rights, safety, infection control, and medication usage.[21]

- You can also complain to your state's Department of Health.

Please use these resources only when absolutely necessary. If you do find it necessary be sure you have a record of what your complaint is, where and when the situation happened, who in the chain of command you went to about it, and what they did (or did not do) about the situation. Keep track of

---

18 Contact information is in Appendix 1 of this book.
19 Contact information is in Appendix 1 of this book
20 Formerly known as JCAHO – Joint Commission on Accreditation of Healthcare Organizations.
21 Contact information is in Appendix 1 of this book

dates and times, and keep copies of anything you have signed or written. If any other outside agencies were involved, such as the police, other hospitals, etc. be sure to keep a careful log of records of those as well. Maybe you will need all of this information, or maybe not. Just keep in mind that it's better to have it and not need it, rather than need it and not have it.

I have a lot of confidence in the mental healthcare system, and I believe that it is very unlikely that you will need to use these resources, but I would be remiss if I didn't include them in this book. In the vast majority of cases problems can be resolved quickly and efficiently within the facility itself.

The following appendices contain listings on the national level (United States), not international or local levels. I strongly recommend that you also look into your state, regional, county, and city mental health resources in addition to these provided in the appendices.

Appendix 1
Contact Information

American Psychiatric Association
Website: www.psych.org
Email: apa@psych.org
Telephone: 1-888-357-7924
Telephone: (outside USA and Canada)
       1-703-907-7300
Address: 1000 Wilson Boulevard
       Suite 1825
       Arlington, VA 22209

American Psychological Association
Website: http://www.apa.org/index.aspx
Telephone: 1-800-374-2721 (or)
       (202) 336-5500
TDD/TTY: (202) 336-6123
Address: 750 First Street, NE
       Washington, DC 20002-4242

Joint Commission
Website: http://www.jointcommission.org/
Telephone: 1-800-994-6610
       (M-F, 8:30 -5 CST)
Address: 1 Renaissance Boulevard
       Oakbrook Terrace, Illinois 60180
       (or)
       601 Thirteenth Street, NW
       Suite 560 South
       Washington, D.C. 20005

National Association of Social Workers
Website: http://www.naswdc.org/
Telephone: (202) 408-8600
Address: 750 First Street, NE
            Suite 700
            Washington, DC 20002-4241

Quality Care Finder *(online)*
Find and compare health care facilities, doctors, plans and suppliers
Website: http://www.medicare.gov/quality-care-finder/

Appendix 2
Mental Health Resources

Brain and Behavior Research Foundation
Their vision is to bring the joy of living to those affected by mental illness – those who are ill and their families and friends.
Website: http://bbrfoundation.org
Telephone: 1-800-829-8289
Address: 60 Cutter Mill Road
            Suite 404
            Great Neck, NY 11021

Internet Mental Health
Internet Mental Health is a free encyclopedia of mental health information created by a Canadian psychiatrist, Dr. Phillip Long.
http://www.mentalhealth.com/

Mental Health America
MHA, the leading advocacy organization addressing the full spectrum of mental and substance use conditions and their effects nationwide, works to inform, advocate and enable access to quality behavioral health services for all Americans.
Website: http://www.mentalhealthamerica.net/
Telephone: 1-800-969-6642
Address: 2000 North Beauregard Street
            6th Floor
            Alexandria, VA 22311

Mental Health Treatment Center Locator
(United States)
http://findtreatment.samhsa.gov/

National Alliance on Mental Illness
NAMI is the National Alliance on Mental Illness, the nation's largest grassroots mental health organization dedicated to building better lives for the millions of Americans affected by mental illness. NAMI advocates for access to services, treatment, supports and research and is steadfast in its commitment to raise awareness and build a community for hope for all of those in need.
Website: http://www.nami.org
Telephone: (703) 524-7600
Help Line: 1-800-950-6264
Address: 3803 N. Fairfax Drive
Suite 100
Arlington, VA 22203

National Institute of Mental Health
The mission of NIMH is to transform the understanding and treatment of mental illnesses through basic and clinical research, paving the way for prevention, recovery, and cure.
Website: http://www.nimh.nih.gov/index.shtml
Telephone: 1-866-615-6464
TTY: 1-866-415-8051
Address: 6001 Executive Boulevard
Room 6200, MSC 9663
Bethesda, MD 20892-9663

National Resource Center on Psychiatric Advance Directives
Psychiatric advance directives are relatively new legal instruments that may be used to document a competent person's specific instructions or preferences regarding future

mental health treatment. Psychiatric advance directives can be used to plan for the possibility that someone may lose capacity to give or withhold informed consent to treatment during acute episodes of psychiatric illness.
Website:http://www.nrc-pad.org/

Psych Central
Large network of resources spanning all forms of mental illness.
Website: http://psychcentral.com/

Substance Abuse and Mental Health Services Administration
SAMHSA's mission is to reduce the impact of substance abuse and mental illness on America's communities.
Website: http://www.samhsa.gov/
Telephone: 1-877- 726-4727
Address: 1 Choke Cherry Road
          Rockville, MD 20857

Appendix 3
Disability Employment Resources

Disability.gov
https://www.disability.gov/employment#map

Enable America
Website: http://www.enableamerica.org/
Telephone: 1 (877) 362-2533
Address: P.O. Box 3031
           Tampa, FL 33601-3031

Getting Hired.com
http://www.gettinghired.com/AdvocacyPartners.aspx
Telephone: (866) 352-7481
Address: 7301 Parkway Drive
           Hanover MD, 21076

Hire Heroes U.S.A. *(Veteran focused)*
Website: https://www.hireheroesusa.org/
Telephone: 1-(866) 915-4376
Address: 100 North Point Center East
           Suite 200
           Alpharetta, GA 30022

Job Accommodation Network
Website:http://askjan.org/indiv/index.htm
Telephone: 1 (800)526-7234
TTY: 1 (877)781-9403

National Business and Disability Council
Website: http://nbdc.com/job_seekers.aspx
Email:lfrancis@viscardicenter.org.
Telephone: (516) 465-1516
Address: 201 I.U. Willets Road
Albertson, New York 11507

Project Vision / Proyecto Vision
Latino focused
Website: http://www.proyectovision.net/index.html
Email: wid@wid.org

Appendix 4
Mental Health Advocacy Resources

Active Minds *(College student focused)*
Website:http://www.activeminds.org/
Telephone: (202) 332-9595
Address: 2001 S Street, NW
        Suite 450
        Washington, DC 20009

Mental Health Advocacy Inc.
Website:http://www.mentalhealthadvocacyinc.org/
Telephone: (919) 809-7253
Address: PO Box 26952
        Raleigh, NC 27611

MindFreedom International
Website: http://www.mindfreedom.org/
Email: office@mindfreedom.org
Telephone: 1-877-623-7743
Address: MindFreedom International
        P.O. Box 11284
        Eugene, OR 97440-3484 USA

National Association For Rights Protection and Advocacy
Website: http://www.narpa.org/
Email: narpa@aol.com
Telephone: (256) 650-6311
Address: P.O. Box 855
        Huntsville, AL 35801

National Disabilities Rights Network
Website: http://www.ndrn.org/index.php
Telephone: (202) 408-9514
TTY: (202) 408-9521
Address: 900 Second Street NE
            Suite 211
            Washington, D.C. 20002

Psych Central's Resource Listings
Website:http://psychcentral.com/resources/Mental_Hea
lth/Advocacy_and_Policy/

Treatment Advocacy Center
Website:http://www.treatmentadvocacycenter.org/
Email: info@treatmentadvocacycenter.org
Telephone: (703) 294-6001
Address: 200 N. Glebe Road
            Suite 730
            Arlington, VA 22203

Appendix 5
Federal HIPAA Law

"HIPAA" (pronounced "hip-uh") stands for **H**ealth **I**nsurance **P**ortability and **A**ccountability **A**ct. Basically, this a federal law that is in place and intended to protect the privacy of patients and their personal medical information. The following is direct information from the official website of the Department of Health and Human Services (as of 2013):

Who Must Follow These Laws?

We call the entities that must follow the HIPAA regulations **"Covered Entities."** *Covered entitites include: Health plans, most health care providers, health care clearinghouses, and the business associates of these entities.*

Who Is Not Required to Follow These Laws?

Many organizations that have health information about you do not have to follow these laws. This would include: Life insurers, employers, worker's compensation carriers, most schools and school districts, law enforcement agencies, many state agencies, many municipal offices.

What Information Is Protected?

Protected information includes: Information that your doctors, nurses and other health care providers put in your medical records, conversations between doctors and nurses about your case, information about you in your health care provider's computer system, billing information about you, and all other health care information about you held by those who must follow these laws.

Covered entities are responsible for keeping your medical information confidential as well as ensuring your information is not given away improperly. Information can only be given on a need to know basis.[22]

What Rights Does The Privacy Rule Give Me Over My Health Information?

Health Insurers and Providers who are covered entities must comply with your right to: Obtain a copy of your own health records, have corrections added to your health information, receive notice of how your health information will be used or shared, decide of you want to give permission to share your information outside of covered entities, receive a report of when and why your information was shared, and file a complaint if you feel your privacy was illegally violated.

Who Among My Family And Friends Can See My Information?

Generally, a covered health care provider or health plan must allow your personal representative to inspect and receive a copy of protected health information about you that the covered health care provider or health plan maintains. A personal representative can be named several ways; state law may affect how a person becomes a personal

---

22 There was a case some years ago where a United States President was hospitalized. Some of the medical staff in the facility who were NOT his caregivers snooped into his medical records purely out of curiosity. Because they did not need to know this information the facility fired the offenders over this invasion of his privacy.

113

representative. If a person can make health care decisions for you using a health care power of attorney, the person is your personal representative.

A provider or plan may choose not to treat a person as your personal representative if the provider or plan reasonably believes that the person might endanger you in situations of domestic violence, abuse, or neglect.

The Privacy Rule does not require a health care provider or health plan to share information with your family or friends, unless they are your personal representatives. The law does permit providers and plans to share information with them in certain circumstances.

A health care provider or health plan may share relevant information with family members or friends involved in your health care or payment for your health care, if you tell the provider or plan that it can do so, or if you do not object to sharing of the information.

For example, if you do not object, your doctor could talk with the friend who goes with you to the hospital or with a family member who pays your medical bill.

A provider or plan may also share relevant information with these persons if, using its professional judgment, it believes that you do not object. For example, if you send your friend to pick up your prescription of medication the pharmacist can assume that you do not object to his being given the medication. Or, as another example, if you are too injured to give permission a provider may share information when it is deemed to be in your best interest.